EARTH CYCLES

EARTH'S WATER CYCLE

by Sally Morgan

Smart Apple Media

Published by Smart Apple Media
P.O. Box 3263, Mankato, Minnesota 56002

Printed in the United States of America at Corporate Graphics, in North Mankato, Minnesota.

Published by arrangement with the Watts Publishing Group Ltd., London.

Library of Congress Cataloging-in-Publication Data
Morgan, Sally, 1957-
   Earth's Water Cycle / by Sally Morgan.
      p. cm. -- (Earth cycles)
   Includes bibliographical references and index.
   Summary: "Discusses the different forms of water and includes diagrams to explain how it is recycled through our planet. Presents how the water cycle is changing due to climate change and suggests ways we can help save water"--Provided by publisher.
   ISBN 978-1-59920-523-6 (library binding)
   1. Water--Juvenile literature. I. Title.
   GB662.3.M675 2012
   553.7--dc22

                              2010030435

Produced for Franklin Watts by
White-Thomson Publishing, Ltd.
Editor: Jean Coppendale
Design: Paul Manning

Picture credits

t = top b = bottom l = left = r = right

1, 4, Shutterstock/Mana Photo; 3b, Shutterstock/Podfoto; 3t, 5, Shutterstock/Sony Ho; 5r, Shutterstock/Steffen Foerster Photography; 6, Shutterstock/Willem Dijkstra; 7m, Shutterstock/B. Howe; 7r, Shutterstock/Pichugin Dmitry; 7b, Shutterstock/Tania Zbrodko; 8, Shutterstock/Algul; 8t, Shutterstock/Robert Paul van Beets; 9l, ECO/Reinhard Dirscherl; 9r, ECO/Steven Kazlowski; 10, Stefan Chabluk; 11l, Shutterstock/Kevin Day; 11r, Shutterstock/Frontpage; 12 background, Shutterstock/Matsonashvili Mikhail; 12l, Shutterstock/Lars Christensen; 13l, Shutterstock/Iofoto; 13m, GDF/Chmury Warstwy; 13r, Shutterstock/Maxphoto; 14, Shutterstock/Tobago Cays; 14r, Shutterstock/Dainis Derics; 15l, ECO/Nicholas and Sherry Lu Aldridge; 15r, Shutterstock/Wolfgang Amri; 16l, Shutterstock/Mauro Rodrigues; 16, Shutterstock/Galushko Sergey; 17, Shutterstock/Jackie Foster; 18, Shutterstock/Cre8tive Images; 19l, Shutterstock/Johnny Lye; 19r, ECO/Reinhard Discherl; 20, Shutterstock/Anton Kossmann; 21bl, Stefan Chabluk; 21r, ECO/Stephen Coyne; 21br, ECO/Wayne Lawler; 22, ECO/Chinch Gryniewicz; 23l, ECO/Wayne Lawler; 23r, ECO/Robert Weight; 24 main, Shutterstock/Andromed; 24l, Shutterstock/Gail Johnson; 25l, Shutterstock/Graham Prentice; 25r, GDF/Earth Sciences and Image Analysis Laboratory, NASA Johnson Space Center; 26, 30, ECO/Steven Kazlowski; 27l, ECO/Sally Morgan; 27bl, ECO/Wayne Lawler; 27r, Shutterstock/Jelica Grkic; 28 main, Shutterstock/ Amp; 29, ECO/Anthony Cooper; 29r, Shutterstock/AGphotographer.
Cover images: main, Shutterstock/Mana Photo; top, Shutterstock/Yegorius; center, Shutterstock/Robert Ranson; bottom, ECO/David Wootton Photography.

Note to parents and teachers

Every effort has been made by the publishers to ensure that the web sites listed on page 32 are suitable for children, that they are of the highest educational value, and that they contain no inappropriate or offensive material. However, because of the nature of the Internet, it is impossible to guarantee that the contents of these sites have not been altered. We strongly advise that Internet access is supervised by a responsible adult.

1371

6-2011

9 8 7 6 5 4 3 2

Contents

Words appearing in **bold**
can be found in the
glossary on pages 30–31.

Earth's Water

Earth is a watery planet. There is so much water on its surface that the earth is sometimes called the "blue planet." The earth is the only planet we know of in the solar system where water exists as a liquid.

▼ The oceans cover an area of about 139 million square miles (360 million sq km). This means that more than 70 percent of the earth's surface is covered by water.

Salt Water

We are used to seeing freshwater in streams, rivers, and lakes, but this is only a tiny fraction of the water on the earth. Almost all of our water is salt water, and it fills the vast oceans.

Q and A

Fresh water

Only 3 percent of the earth's water is freshwater. A little less than 70 percent of the freshwater is locked up as ice in **ice caps** and **glaciers**, while another 30 percent is in the ground. Less than 0.3 percent of freshwater is found in lakes and rivers.

Q How did the oceans become salty?

A Millions of years ago, there were no oceans because the earth's surface was too hot for water to exist. Volcanic eruptions produced steam, and this cooled to form rain that filled the oceans. The water became salty from the **minerals** in the rocks and volcanic ash.

▼ Niagara Falls on the Niagara River is the most powerful waterfall in North America.

▲ Clouds of dust and steam rise from a volcanic eruption in Hawaii as lava flows into the Pacific Ocean.

Losing and Gaining Water

Oceans, lakes, and rivers are continually losing and gaining water, and this drives the **water cycle**. Water moves from the surface of the oceans into the **atmosphere**. From there, the water falls to the earth as rain, hail, sleet, or snow. Once on the ground, some of the water enters streams and rivers and returns to the oceans. The rest of the water soaks into the ground.

Solids, Liquids, and Gases

Water is unusual because it is found naturally in three different forms—as a solid called ice, a liquid called water, and a gas known as water **vapor**.

Solids, such as ice and rock, are hard and do not change shape when you move them. A liquid flows and takes the shape of its container; for example, milk can be poured from a carton into a glass. Gases have no fixed shape or **volume**. The air around us contains a mixture of gases including **nitrogen**, **oxygen**, water vapor, and **carbon dioxide**.

Freezing and Melting

When water is cooled to $32°F$ ($0°C$), liquid water changes into solid ice. This is called freezing. When ice is heated, the heat **energy** causes the ice to melt and turn into a liquid.

▶ Water freezes when its temperature falls to 32°F (0°C).

Q and A

Evaporation

Water vapor forms when liquid water is heated and **evaporates**. For example, puddles of water quickly disappear when the sun comes out. The sun heats the water in the puddle, and this causes the liquid water to change into a vapor.

▼ Laundry dries when water evaporates in the sun.

Q What is the boiling point of water at the top of Mount Everest?

A It is 158°F (70°C). At sea level, water boils at 212°F (100°C). However, the air is much thinner at the top of Everest, so the water boils at a lower temperature.

▲ Mount Everest, 29,029 ft. (8,848 m) high

Condensation

Condensation takes place when a gas such as water vapor is cooled and forms a liquid. For example, droplets of water appear on a window when warm air comes into contact with a cold window pane. Evaporation and condensation are the key processes in the water cycle.

condensation

◄ Water has condensed on the surface of this cold can.

Fresh and Salt Water

There is plenty of salt water on the earth, but supplies of freshwater are limited.

Solvent

Water is a **solvent**. This means that it **dissolves** substances. Sugar dissolves in water, for example. Water contains many dissolved substances, such as **sodium, calcium**, and **chloride**, that it picks up as it passes through the ground. Freshwater is water in which there is less than 3 parts per thousand (ppt) of salt. Most freshwater has less than 0.5 ppt of salt. If there is more than 3 ppt of salt present, then it is called salt water. Seawater has an average of 35 ppt of salt.

▼ The water in the Dead Sea is almost 30 percent salt. All this salt makes floating very easy. The Dead Sea is the only place in the world where you can float on the water and read a book!

Salt deposits around the Dead Sea

Q and A

Living in Salt Water

Animals that live in the oceans have **adapted** to living in salt water. For example, many have special **glands** that remove the excess salt from their bodies. People and other animals that live on land cannot drink salt water because our bodies, especially our **kidneys**, cannot deal with the salt. We rely on freshwater.

Q Which fish is born in freshwater but lives most of its life in salt water?

A The salmon. This amazing fish is born in freshwater streams and rivers. It spends the first year or so of its life in freshwater and then swims out to sea. Several years later, it returns to the place where it was born to breed.

◀ Turtles get rid of excess salt in their bodies by producing salty tears from the salt gland behind their eyes.

▲ Sockeye salmon

Removing the Salt

In the Middle East and other places where freshwater is in short supply, **desalination** plants remove the salt from seawater. The water is boiled, so that the water evaporates and the salt is left behind. Unfortunately, this process uses a lot of energy, so producing freshwater in this way is expensive and bad for the environment.

Cycling Water

Water is continually moving through the water cycle and changing from liquid to gas and back again. Amazingly, the total amount of water on the earth stays about the same. This means that the water that was present on the planet millions of years ago is still here and has been recycled over and over again.

2
Water exists in the atmosphere as water vapor. High in the atmosphere, the water condenses and forms clouds.

3
Water falls to the ground as rain, snow, sleet, or hail.

1
Water evaporates from all surfaces, including the oceans, and forms water vapor in the atmosphere.

5
Some water runs off the land and enters streams and lakes. Some streams form rivers, and rivers empty into the oceans.

4
Some of the water soaks into the ground and becomes **groundwater**, moving through rocks. It may come out again as **springwater** or be pumped from wells.

Q and A

Q Which river empties the largest amount of freshwater into the ocean?

A The Amazon. This river contributes about one-fifth of all the freshwater that enters the oceans from rivers. During the rainy season, more than 79,251,600 gallons (300,000 m³) of freshwater from the Amazon enter the ocean every second.

▲ Water evaporates from the surfaces of trees and rivers. Here, the evaporated water has condensed to form mist.

▲ The Amazon River

Water in the Atmosphere

A lot of water is held in the atmosphere. If all the water in the atmosphere rained down at once, it would produce about 1 inch (2.5 cm) of rain over the entire surface of the earth.

Humid Air

Humidity is the amount of water vapor in the air. Warm air holds a lot of water, so when it rains on warm days, the air becomes very humid. Cold air tends to be drier, as it cannot hold much water vapor.

Clouds and Condensation

The key process in cloud formation is condensation. Warm air is less **dense** than cold air, so it rises into the atmosphere. It is much cooler higher up in the atmosphere, so the warm water vapor cools, condenses, and forms water droplets. High in the atmosphere, it is so cold that the water forms ice.

▲ **Cumulus** clouds are often seen on warm days. They are a sign of fair weather.

▶ A rainbow appears when there is sunshine and rain because the sunlight splits into many different colors as it passes through water droplets.

Making Clouds

Clouds form when water droplets join with other particles in the air, such as dust, ash, or smoke, to form cloud droplets. Clouds change shape all the time as water evaporates and then condenses. The three main shapes of clouds are called cumulus, **cirrus**, and **stratus**.

Q What is a mackerel sky?

A This is a pattern of clouds that looks like the scales on a mackerel fish. Some people also call these patterns "sheep clouds" because they look like a flock of fluffy sheep. The appearance of these clouds may mean that the weather is about to change.

◄ Cirrus clouds are high clouds made of ice crystals. They form when there is good weather.

▼ Stratus clouds are low, sheet-like clouds that cover the sky. These clouds are associated with cloudy days, and they may bring drizzle or rain.

▲ Mackerel sky

13

Falling to the Ground

A water **molecule** spends about 10 days in the atmosphere before falling to the ground. Clouds hold a lot of water droplets, but individually they are too small to fall. For rain to fall, the droplets must get larger until they are too heavy to be held in the cloud. This happens when droplets bump into each other and join up.

Precipitation

The water that falls to the ground is called **precipitation**. Most falls as rain, but some falls as sleet, hail, or snow. Snowflakes are made up of tiny ice crystals stuck together. Snowflakes can melt by the time they reach the ground, but if the air is cold enough, they fall as snow.

▶ Towering **cumulonimbus** clouds bring thunder and lightning and heavy rainfall.

▼ Snowfall is common during the winter months in the northern **temperate** regions.

Climates

The pattern of rainfall varies around the world, and this creates the **climates**. In the **tropics**, rain usually falls all year round. Temperate regions have **seasonal climates** with less rain falling in summer. **Desert climates** have very little rain.

Wind and Rain

In many places, winds bring rain. For example, the **monsoon season** in India occurs when the wind blows off the Indian Ocean and brings with it **torrential rain**. Then the wind direction changes. It blows off the land, and the weather becomes hot and dry.

Q Why does more rain fall on mountains?

A Mountains force warm, moist air to rise. As the air rises, it cools, and the water condenses and falls as rain. In winter, the rain may fall as snow.

▲ Mountain skiing

◀ During the monsoon season in countries such as Vietnam, many inches (cm) of rain can fall in a short period of time, causing **flash floods**.

15

Evaporation

Water evaporates from all surfaces—oceans, plants, puddles, buildings, and even our skin.

Evaporation is driven by the heat from the sun. Heat energy makes water molecules move more quickly, and some evaporate from the surface of water. When water evaporates from the surface of the oceans, the salt is left behind.

▼ These workers are collecting salt that has been left behind in salt ponds after the water has evaporated.

Q and A

Humidity

The amount of evaporation that takes place depends on factors such as the temperature of the air, wind speed, and humidity. For example, more water evaporates when temperatures are high. High humidity slows evaporation because the air can only hold a certain amount of water. Once the air is **saturated**, no more water can evaporate. However, wind helps to increase evaporation because it carries humid air away and usually replaces it with drier air.

Loss or Gain?

In some places, there is more evaporation than condensation. Over the oceans, for example, more water evaporates than falls as rain. This evaporated water is the source of much of the water in the atmosphere. Winds blow moist air from the oceans over the land, where the water falls as rain. On land, more water falls to the ground than is evaporated from surfaces. Some runs off into rivers and reenters the oceans.

Q How does evaporation keep us cool?

A Water needs heat energy to evaporate. When water evaporates from the surface of our skin, it takes heat from the skin, and this makes us feel cooler. When we are hot, we drink water to replace the water lost by evaporation.

▲ Drinking water after exercise replaces water lost by evaporation.

▼ Fog forms when humid air comes into contact with a cold surface. The water vapor condenses and clouds form near the ground.

17

Plants and Water

Plants have a key role in the water cycle because evaporation from the surfaces of plants makes up 10 percent of all evaporation into the atmosphere.

Water for Support

Water is essential to plants. Plants use water as a form of support. If a plant loses too much water, its leaves collapse. This is called wilting. If water is not given quickly, the plant dies. Water is also used in **photosynthesis**, the process by which plants make food.

► Plants take in water from the soil through their roots. It is carried up the stem to the leaves, from where it evaporates. Evaporation from a plant is called **transpiration**.

3
Water evaporates from the surface of the leaves.

2
Water travels up through the plant via the stem.

1
Water is absorbed by the plant's roots.

Q and A

Rain Forests

Rain forest trees grow close together to form a thick **canopy** over the forest. As a result, about half the rainfall never reaches the ground. The rain lands on the leaves of the canopy, where it evaporates back into the atmosphere to fall again as rain. The water that does reach the ground is held by the soil and released slowly into streams. When the forests are cleared (see page 27), the local water cycle is disrupted. There is less transpiration, which means less rain. Without the protective tree cover, the soil is washed away in heavy rains and there is more flooding.

▼ Rain forest trees hold lots of water and protect the soil from being washed away.

Q How do cacti survive in the desert?

A Cacti do not have leaves; instead, they have spines. This reduces transpiration and stops animals from eating them. They also have a thick **cuticle** over their stem to reduce water loss. Some cacti, such as the cardon cactus, can store water in their stems.

▲ Desert cacti

Underground Water

More than 33 percent of the world's freshwater is stored in the ground.

Groundwater

Water seeps through the soil, moving along cracks and filling the spaces between soil particles. Some of the water is taken up by plant roots, but the rest moves deeper still. Eventually, the ground holds as much water as is possible with all the spaces filled with water. When this happens, the ground is described as being saturated.

Water Table

The top of the saturated zone is called the **water table**. If you dig a hole down to the water table, the bottom of the hole will fill with water. The height of the water table varies, depending on the weather. After wet weather, the water table is high in the ground.

▲ In some places, water pours through holes in the ground to form underground rivers.

Aquifers

Rocks such as chalk and sandstone contain many pores, or holes, that hold water. These water-holding rocks are called **aquifers**. Water moves down through cracks and pores in the rocks until it reaches a layer, such as clay, through which it cannot pass.

Springs

A spring is a place where water bubbles up from the ground. It forms where the aquifer reaches the surface and the water can escape, for example, on a hillside, where the slope cuts down through an aquifer.

Q What is fossil water?

A This is water that has been locked up in underground rocks beneath the desert. Scientists estimate that some fossil water may be 40,000 years old.

▲ Watering crops in the desert

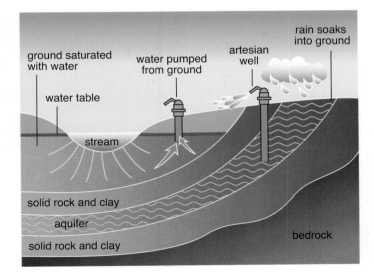

▲ If there are no springs, water can be reached by digging a well. Some wells need a pump to bring the water to the surface. In an **artesian well** (right), the water is under pressure, so it gushes from the ground and there is no need for a pump.

Glaciers

Glaciers are huge rivers of ice that form in mountains and the polar regions. On glaciers, it is so cold that the snow does not melt. Instead, it builds up to form a thick mass of ice.

On the Move

When a glacier is about 65 feet (20 m) thick, it becomes so heavy that the ice starts to move downhill. The ice at the top moves more quickly than the ice at the bottom. Glaciers are not pure ice, as they contain lots of pieces of rock. These rocks rub against the ground and wear away the sides of the mountain as the glacier moves.

▶ A glacier extends down a valley in the Himalayas. It looks dirty because of all the rock on and in the ice.

Q and A

Expanding and Shrinking

In winter, glaciers expand, often moving by a yard (meter) or so a day, but they shrink in summer. When the ice melts, the bits of rock are dropped and this forms a pile of rock called a **moraine**.

▲ A valley that once had a glacier has a "U" shape because the ice has worn away its sides. In spring, the ice at the end of the glacier starts to melt and the water runs off to form fast-flowing mountain streams.

Q Which mountain range is buried under a glacier?

A The Transantarctic Mountains in **Antarctica**. These mountains stretch across Antarctica for a distance of 2,175 miles (3,500 km), dividing East Antarctica from West Antarctica. The mountains rise to 14,764 feet (4,500 m) above sea level, but they are buried by the huge Antarctic **ice sheet**, and just their tips show above the ice.

▲ The Trans-antarctic Mountains in Antarctica

Ice Age

Thousands of years ago, during the last **ice age**, the earth was much colder, and the ice caps and glaciers expanded to cover one-third of all the land. Today, they cover less than 10 percent of the land, but they still store 70 percent of the world's freshwater.

23

Rivers

Much of the water falling on land becomes part of the groundwater, but a small amount enters rivers.

The Source of a River

Rivers start life as small streams. The source of the water may be a spring on a hillside, the meltwater from a glacier, or melting snow in spring. The water in a stream flows quickly, tumbling over rocks and wearing them away.

Streams Become Rivers

As more water enters a stream, it becomes larger and it is called a river. A river carries a lot of **sediment** that has been picked up by the water, for example clay and **silt**, as well as leaves and twigs and other debris.

▲ The water in streams tumbles down the mountainside.

▼ The water flows more slowly in this large river.

Meanders

A **mature river** is surrounded by a **flood plain**. This is the flat land on either side of the river that floods after heavy rains. The water flows quickly along some stretches, wearing away the banks. But it may also flow more slowly in other places, where it drops some of its sediment to form **sand banks**. This creates bends in the river called **meanders**. Eventually, a river reaches the sea.

▼ This river is meandering across its flood plain.

Q What is an estuary?

A An **estuary** is the point where a river enters the sea. The flow of water slows down and the river drops the sediment that it is carrying. The sediment builds up into **mudflats**. The water is **brackish**—neither fresh nor salty but a mixture of the two.

sea

coastline

estuary

river

▲ A river estuary

25

Water and Climate Change

The water cycle has been taking place for millions of years. Although the amount of water on earth has not varied, the patterns of rainfall and the amount of water locked up in ice has changed many times in the past. Changes are taking place now and they have been caused by **global warming**.

▼ The ice sheets of the polar regions are shrinking, and this is threatening the habitats of polar animals such as polar bears.

Retreating Glaciers

As the earth gets warmer, more of the world's glaciers are retreating, and the water that was once ice has melted and is now in the sea. The oceans are becoming warmer and they are expanding. This is because warm water occupies a larger space than the same volume of cold water. This, together with more meltwater, means that sea levels are rising.

Deforestation

When forests are cleared, there is less transpiration, and this leads to less rain in places that once had plenty. There are no tree roots to hold the soil in place, so there is more **soil erosion**. The water runs straight off the land and causes flooding.

Q How quickly are the glaciers retreating?

A Most glaciers are retreating at a rate of many yards (meters) a year. Many will disappear in the next 20 to 30 years. Glaciers in the central and eastern Himalayas could disappear by 2040, while in Glacier National Park in Montana, only 30 of the original 150 glaciers still remain. Most of the ice has retreated in the last 20 years.

◀ **Deforestation** (top) has led to soil erosion. Now the stream (below) is clogged up with silt.

▲ Glacier National Park, Montana

27

Saving Water

As the world's population increases, both farming and industry will have to expand to meet the extra demand. This will lead to more water usage. However, there is only a limited amount of water. We need to conserve water so that we do not run out of it.

Climate Change

Climate change has made things worse. Climates around the world are becoming less predictable, and this affects some places more than others. There may be floods one year and droughts the next, putting the survival of many plants and animals at risk.

Collecting Water

In many places, more rain falls in winter, but the demand for water increases in summer. To overcome this problem, **reservoirs** (large lakes) are built in areas with high rainfall to trap the water and store it for use later in the year.

▼ In this village in India, every house collects water from the roofs and stores it in large tanks.

▼ Crops have to be watered regularly. Otherwise, the plants die and the crop is lost.

Q and A

Water Sense

There are many ways to reduce our use of water. Every day you could make a difference. For example, turn off faucets as quickly as possible, take a shower rather than a bath, and collect bathwater to water house plants. Plants in the garden need watering too, so collect water when it rains using rain barrels and other containers, and use this to water plants.

Q How much water does a person living in a more **economically developed** country use each day?

A In the United States, the average person uses 105 gallons (400 L) or more of water a day. A person living in a less economically developed country, such as Tanzania in Africa, may use only 5 gallons (20 L) a day.

◄ Use water from bathtubs and sinks to water plants in the garden.

► Leaving faucets running wastes a lot of water.

Glossary

adapt to change to suit the environment

Antarctica a very cold continent at the South Pole

aquifer a water-holding rock

artesian well a well where water rises to the surface without the need for a pump

atmosphere the layer of gases around the earth

brackish water that is slightly salty

calcium a mineral found in rocks, bones, and shells

canopy the branches of trees that form a "roof" over a forest

carbon dioxide a colorless gas found in the air

chloride a part of common salt

cirrus a high-altitude wispy cloud made of ice crystals

climate the regular pattern of weather in an area

climate change the gradual shift in the world's climates due to global warming

condensation the change from a gas to liquid state

cumulonimbus a towering dark mass of cumulus cloud associated with thunder and lightning

cumulus fluffy low-altitude cloud

cuticle the waxy covering over a leaf or stem which is particularly thick in a cactus

deforestation widespread cutting and clearing of trees in a forest

dense heavy, compact

desalination the process of producing freshwater from salt water

desert climate a climate of very dry places where there is little rainfall

dissolve to make or become liquid; for example, sugar dissolves in water to form a sugary liquid or solution.

economically developed having industry and wealth

energy the power to do work

estuary where a river enters the sea

evaporate to change from liquid to gas

flash flood a sudden flood caused by very heavy rainfall over a short period of time

flood plain low-lying land beside a river that often floods

glacier a frozen mass of ice that forms in cold places such as mountains and polar regions

gland a group of cells that form an organ in the body that releases substances

global warming the gradual increase of the surface temperature of the earth

groundwater water found in rocks and soil in the ground

humidity the amount of water vapor in the air

ice age a period in which the earth was much colder and the ice caps and glaciers covered more land

ice cap the thick mass of ice at the poles

ice sheet a large, flat covering of ice

kidney an organ in the body that filters the blood to get rid of waste substances

mature river a river in which water flows slowly

meander a bend in a river

minerals naturally occurring substances in the ground

molecule the smallest particle of a substance

monsoon season a period of the year when winds blow off the ocean and bring torrential rain to countries in South Asia

moraine piles or areas of rock dropped from a glacier

mudflats low-lying, muddy land that is found in estuaries and along coasts

nitrogen a gas found in the atmosphere

oxygen a colorless gas found in the atmosphere

photosynthesis the process by which plants make their own food using light energy, carbon dioxide, and water

precipitation the water that falls to the ground, as rain, hail, sleet, or snow

reservoir a large man-made lake where water is stored

sand bank a ridge of sand that forms in a river or near a shore

saturated holding as much water as possible

seasonal climate a climate with regular changes in the patterns of weather

sediment small particles of clay, silt, and sand carried by water

silt tiny particles of clay and sand picked up by flowing water

sodium a mineral that joins with chloride to form salt

soil erosion the wearing away of soil by water and wind

solvent a liquid that will dissolve another substance

springwater water that emerges from the ground

stratus low, gray clouds

temperate region an area of the world that has a climate with moderate or mild temperatures and seasonal changes

torrential rain very heavy rain

transpiration the evaporation of water from the leaves of a plant

tropics hot and often wet regions of the world near the equator

vapor the gas of a substance that usually exists as a liquid

volume the amount of space occupied by an object

water cycle the continual circulation of water between the oceans, atmosphere, and land, involving condensation and evaporation

water table the level in the ground where the rocks are saturated with water

Further Reading

Barker, Geoff. *Water*. World at Risk. Smart Apple Media, 2010.

Gardner, Robert. *Earth's Cycles: Green Science Projects about the Water Cycle, Photosynthesis, and More*. Enslow, 2011.

Laidlaw, Jill. *Water*. Sustaining Our Environment. Amicus, 2011.

Web Sites

Southwest Florida Water Management District Kids' Page
http://www.swfwmd.state.fl.us/education/kids/
Learn about water, how the water cycle affects weather and storms, and find conservation ideas for your school.

USGS Water Science for Schools
http://ga.water.usgs.gov/edu/
The USGS provides extensive information about the water cycle, with quizzes and activities.

Water Conservation around the House
http://www.ecokids.ca/pub/eco_info/topics/water/water/index.cfm
EcoKids Canada provides games and activities that promote water conservation at home.

Index